FIRST STEPS

Sounds Fun 1

S. Cassin & D. Smith

Illustrated by A. Rodger

Collins: Glasgow and London

© 1980 C.E.M.A.
0 00 197010 0
First Impression 1980
Printed in Great Britain

All rights reserved. No part of this publication may be reproduced, stored in a retrieval system, or transmitted, in any form or by any means, electronic, mechanical, photocopying, recording or otherwise, without prior permission of the copyright owners.

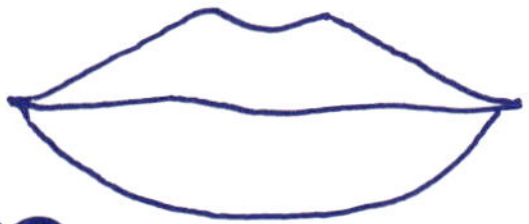

m outh

m onkey

m an

m ilk

m ug

mighty mouse munches macaroni

m oney

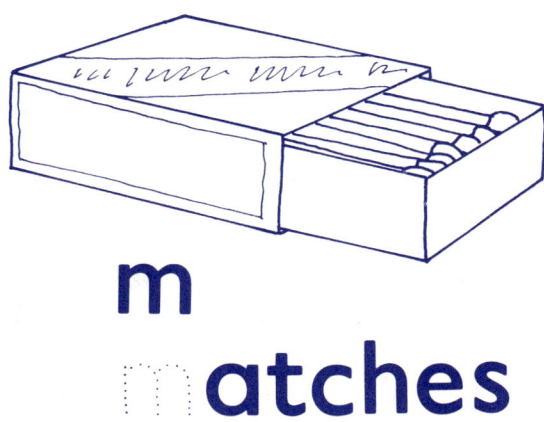
m atches

1 Talk about the pictures and repeat the words while listening for the **m** sound.
2 Trace the big **m** with a finger, then write **m** over the dotted letters. Read the word each time.
3 Read the phrase and learn it. Colour the pictures.
Further activities: 1 Make an **m** tray. 2 Look for **m** words and listen for the sound, e.g. machine, mountain, music, marmalade, moth.

dog domino dot

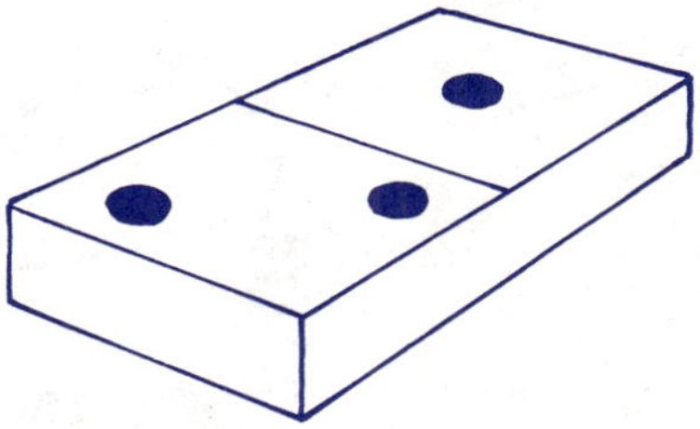

daisy **d** doll

diddle daddle duck dives deeply

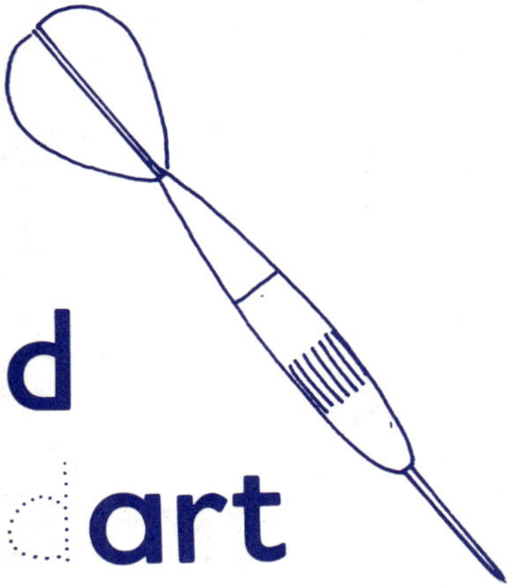

dart door donkey

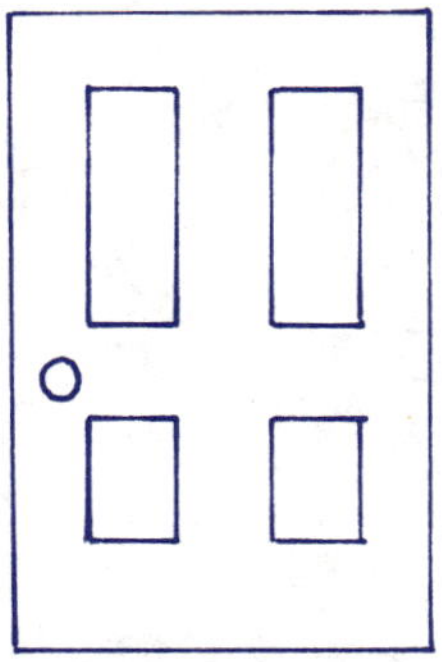

1 Talk about the pictures and repeat the words while listening for the **d** sound.
2 Trace the big **d** with a finger, then write **d** over the dotted letters. Read the word each time.
3 Read the phrase and learn it. Colour the pictures.
Further activities: **1** Make a **d** book.   **2** Look for **d** words and listen for the sound, e.g. dinosaur, dinner, dandelion, dance, dumper.

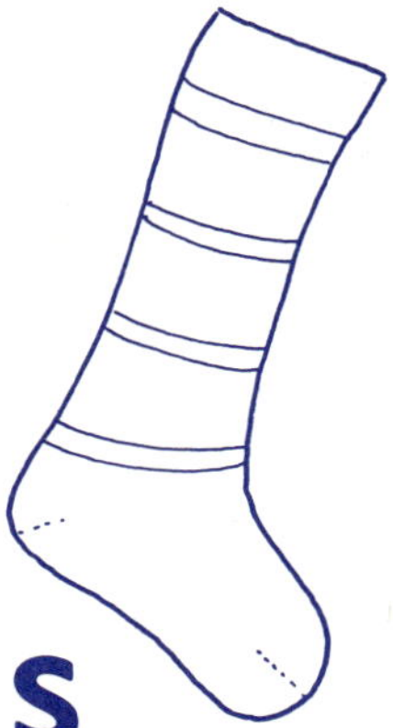

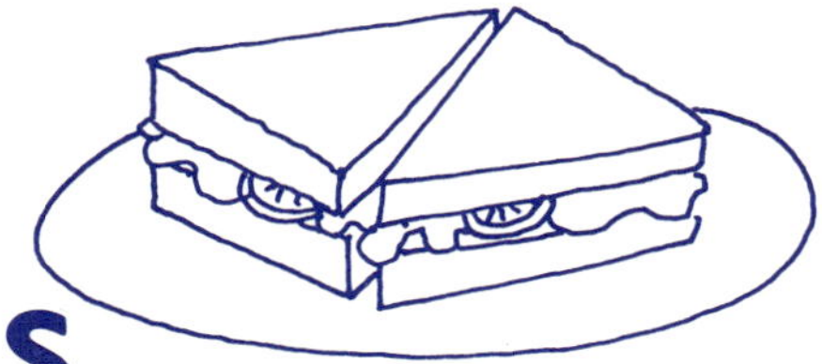

soldier **s**ock **s**andwich

S

sun

supersonic seal sings songs

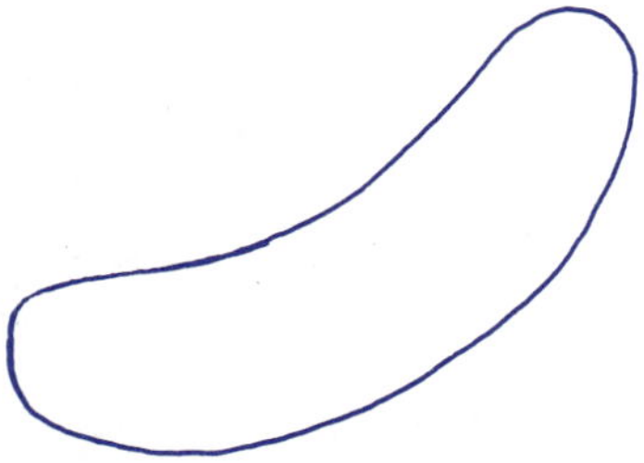

sausage

soap

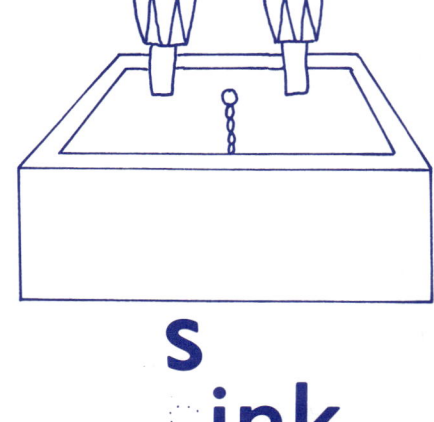
sink

1 Talk about the pictures and repeat the words while listening for the **s** sound.
2 Trace the big **s** with a finger, then write **s** over the dotted letters. Read the word each time.
3 Read the phrase and learn it. Colour the pictures.

Further activities: **1** Make an **s** tray.   **2** Make a big sun with card and colour it yellow. Write **s** on it and hang it from the ceiling.   **3** Look for **s** words and listen for the sound, e.g. salt, sink, sailor, submarine.

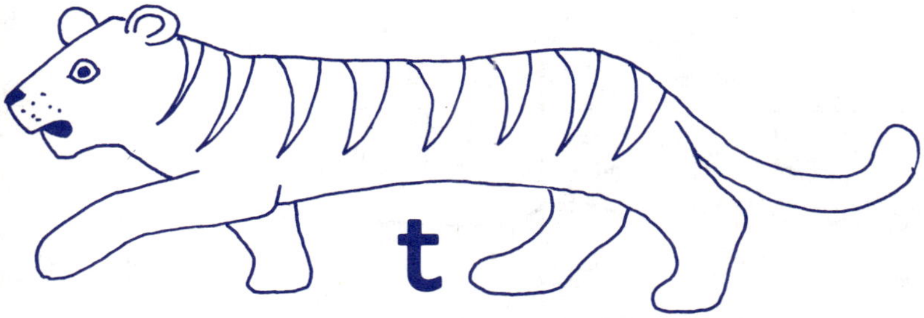

t iger

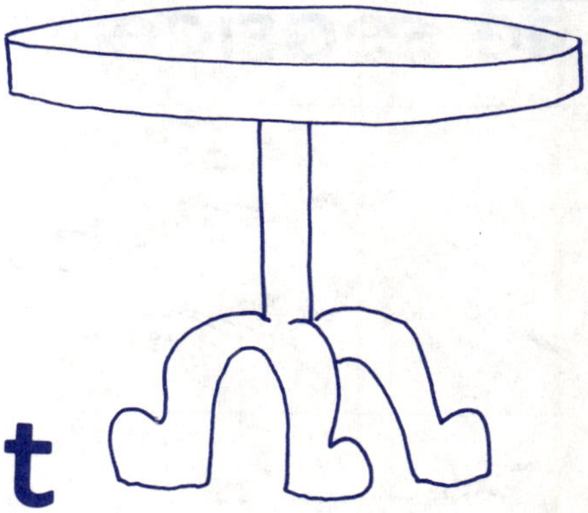

t able

t owel

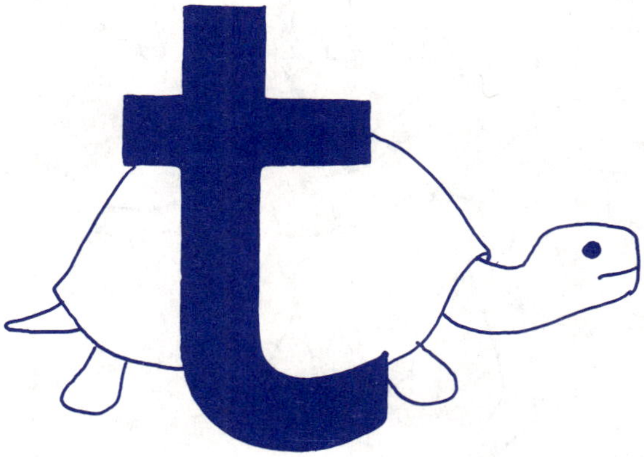

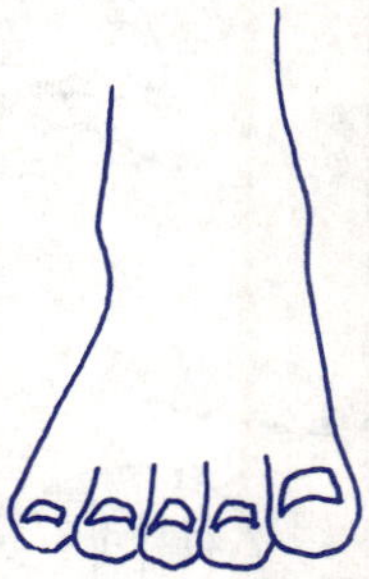

t oes

tittle tattle tortoise tiptoes to town

t eddy

t omato

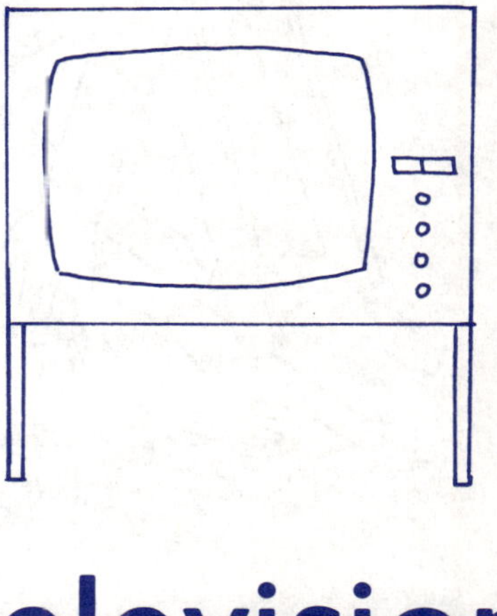

t elevision

1 Talk about the pictures and repeat the words while listening for the **t** sound.
2 Trace the big **t** with a finger, then write **t** over the dotted letters. Read the word each time.
3 Read the phrase and learn it. Colour the pictures.
Further activities: 1 Make a **t** book.   2 Look for **t** words and listen for the sound, e.g. telescope, tunnel, tent, torch.

The seaside

1. Talk about the picture and ask questions about what is happening, e.g. Where is daddy? What can you see flying in the sky?
2. Talk about the sounds some of the objects would be making and try to make some of these sounds.
3. Ask questions about sounds, e.g. Does daddy make a noise when he's sleeping? What kind of noise does the ice cream man make?
4. Colour the picture.

Pillow Penny Pie
Peg Pan
pet penguin picks pockets
Pear Pig

1 Talk about the pictures and repeat the words while listening for the **p** sound.
2 Trace the big **p** with a finger, then write **p** over the dotted letters. Read the word each time.
3 Read the phrase and learn it. Colour the pictures.

Further activities: 1 Make a **p** tray. 2 Look for **p** words and listen for the sound, e.g. pepper, puppy, pirates, puppet. 3 Say this tongue twister: Peter Piper picked a peck of pickled pepper.

c

comb

caterpillar

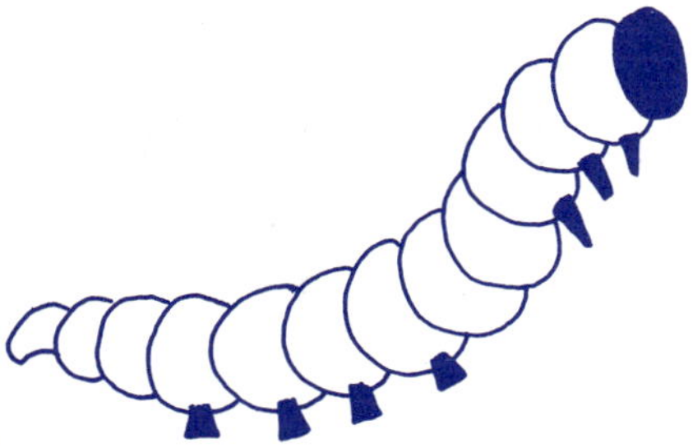

camel

cat

cake

cup

car

careful cow collects caramels

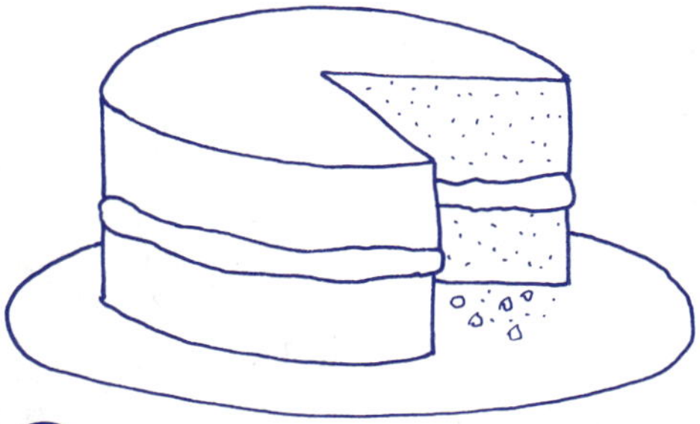

1 Talk about the pictures and repeat the words while listening for the **c** sound.
2 Trace the big **c** with a finger, then write **c** over the dotted letters. Read the word each time.
3 Read the phrase and learn it. Colour the pictures.

Further activities: 1 Make a **c** book. 2 Look for **c** words and listen for the sound, e.g. cushion, corner, camera, coffee, cotton, cod, comic.

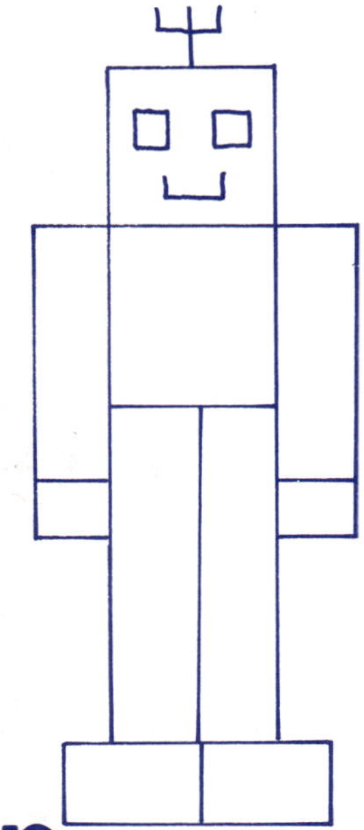

robot

roundabout

rattle

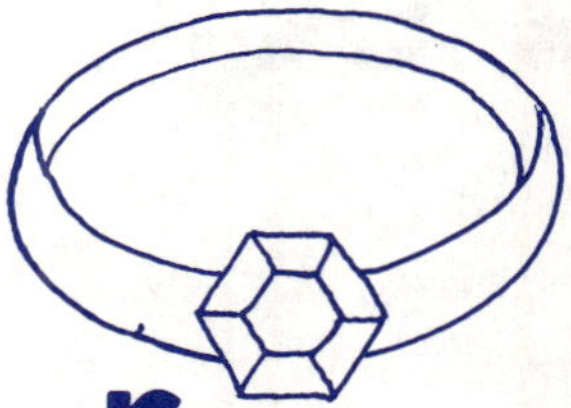

ring

roaring rabbit robs red radishes

rake

rose

rain

1 Talk about the pictures and repeat the words while listening for the **r** sound.
2 Trace the big **r** with a finger, then write **r** over the dotted letters. Read the word each time.
3 Read the phrase and learn it. Colour the pictures.

Further activities: 1 Make an **r** tray. 2 Look for **r** words and listen for the sound, e.g. red, ribbon, ride, road, rock, robber, railway.

n
neck

n
nest

n
nose

n
nail

nasty newt nibbles newspaper

n
net

n
nut

n
needle

1 Talk about the pictures and repeat the words while listening for the **n** sound.
2 Trace the big **n** with a finger, then write **n** over the dotted letters. Read the word each time.
3 Read the phrase and learn it. Colour the pictures.

Further activities: 1 Make an **n** book. 2 Look for **n** words and listen for the sound, e.g. note, nip, nettle, nannie, name.

In the street

1 Talk about the picture and ask questions, e.g. What is the man on the bicycle doing? Is it busy like this when we go to town?

2 Talk about the sounds in a busy street. Ask questions, e.g. If you were standing there on the pavement what would you hear?

3 Colour the picture.

Further activities: **1** Stand outside your house and listen for sounds.   **2** Paint a picture of a busy street.

1 Talk about the pictures and name the objects.
2 Listen for the first sound of each name, and repeat the words.
3 Look at the pictures down the middle of the page with their sound written on them.
4 Point to words with the same sound, then draw a line from each picture to the sound in the middle.
5 Colour the pictures.
Further activities: Cut pictures from a catalogue and make a page for **r, t, d, p.**

goal

goat

girl

gun

goofy gorilla gaily gallops

gate

garage

1 Talk about the pictures and repeat the words while listening for the **g** sound.
2 Trace the big **g** with a finger, then write **g** over the dotted letters. Read the word each time.
3 Read the phrase and learn it. Colour the pictures.
Further activities: Look for **g** words and listen for the sound, e.g. gas, goose, game, go, galleon, gift, guest.

b
butterfly

b
bike

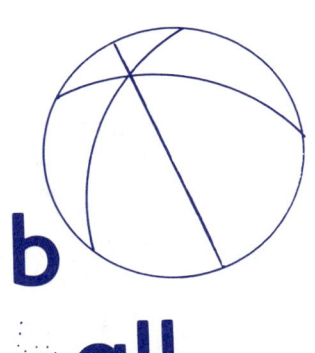
b
ball

b
banana

big bouncy bear bursts balloons

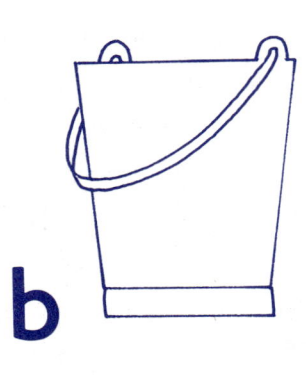
b
bucket

b
button

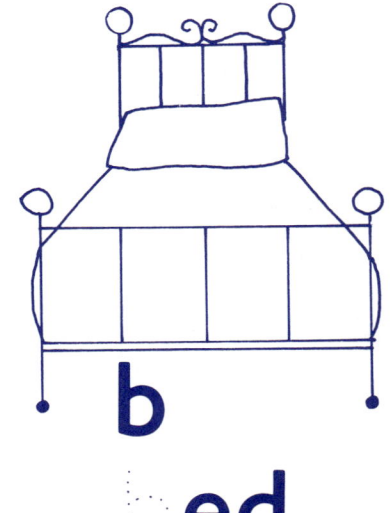
b
bed

1 Talk about the pictures and repeat the words while listening for the **b** sound.
2 Trace the big **b** with a finger, then write **b** over the dotted letters. Read the word each time.
3 Read the phrase and learn it. Colour the pictures.
Further activities: **1** Make a **b** badge.   **2** Look for **b** words and listen for the sound, e.g. beat, bag, bottle, bean, beetroot, big, boat, bottom, balance.

foolish fox follows footsteps

1 Talk about the pictures and repeat the words while listening for the **f** sound.
2 Trace the big **f** with a finger, then write **f** over the dotted letters. Read the word each time.
3 Read the phrase and learn it. Colour the pictures.
Further activities: **1** Make an **f** tray. **2** Cut out a big fish and stick pictures beginning with **f** on it. **3** Look for more **f** words, e.g. feather, fireman, fat, feel, farm, farmer, fall, face.

l eaf

l orry

l ighthouse

lazy lion lifts logs

l eg

l adder

l amp

l ollipop

1 Talk about the pictures and repeat the words while listening for the l sound.
2 Trace the big l with a finger, then write l over the dotted letters. Read the word each time.
3 Read the phrase and learn it. Colour the pictures.

Further activities: 1 Make a lighthouse with a squeezy bottle – cover it with paper and stick l pictures on it. 2 Look for more l words, e.g. loop, long, late, laugh, lady, listen.

In the kitchen

1 Talk about the picture and ask questions, e.g. Is this our kitchen? Why not? What is the postman doing? If you were 'standing in the picture' what sounds would you hear? Are they loud or soft sounds?

2 Colour the picture.

Further activities: 1 Make a Kitchen Book by cutting out pictures from magazines and sticking them on paper. 2 Listen for sounds in your kitchen.

Rhyming sounds

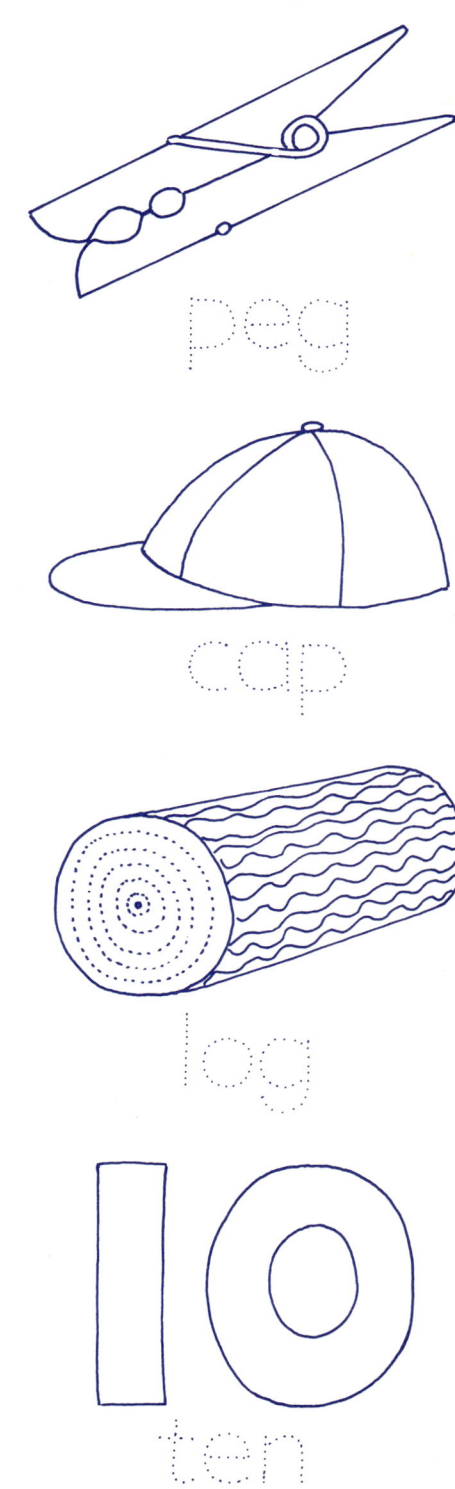

1 Talk about the objects and say the words. Ask your child if any words have the same sound, e.g. tap and cap.

2 Point to the rhyming pairs and join them with a line.

3 Write over the dotted words and colour the pictures.

Further activities: 1 Cut out pictures of words that rhyme, about 3 of each sound, and make cards to play rhyming snap. 2 Say these words and listen to the rhyme: cat – hat; pan – man; dad – sad; jam – ham; net – jet; bed – red.

1 Talk about the pictures, naming the objects.

2 Listen for the first sound of each name. Find the sound in the circle and point to it. Then draw a line from the picture to the sound.

3 Colour the pictures.

Further activities: Cut out pictures from magazines or catalogues and make a page each for **m, n, g, l, b, f, c, p.**

19

hammer

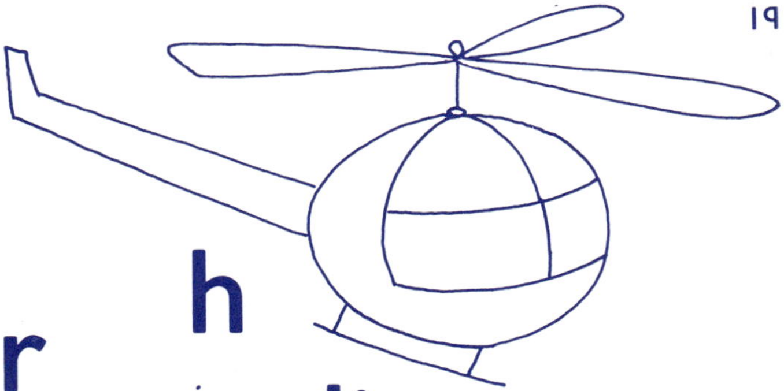

helicopter

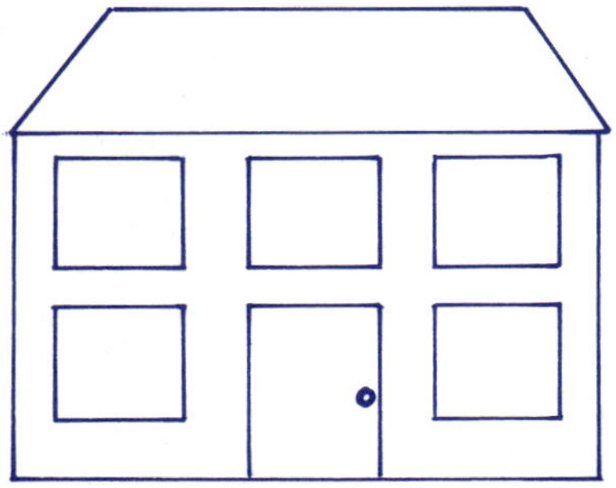

house

hen

happy hedgehog hurries home

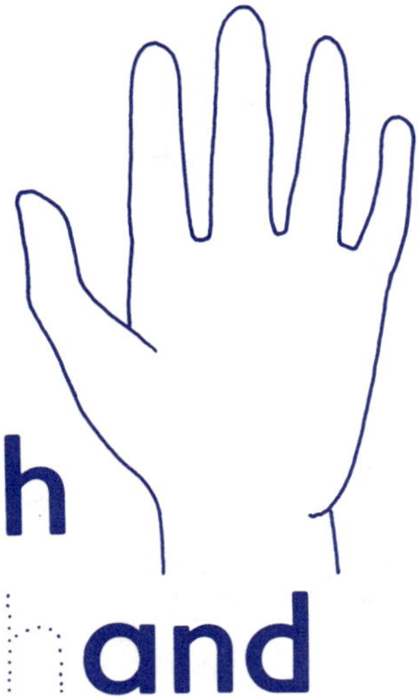

hand

hat

horse

1 Talk about the pictures and repeat the words while listening for the **h** sound.
2 Trace the big **h** with a finger, then write **h** over the dotted letters. Read the word each time.
3 Read the phrase and learn it. Colour the pictures.

Further activities: **1** Make a house from an old cereal box and stick **h** words in the windows. **2** Look for more **h** words, e.g. hippopotamus, happy, hedge, held, hole.

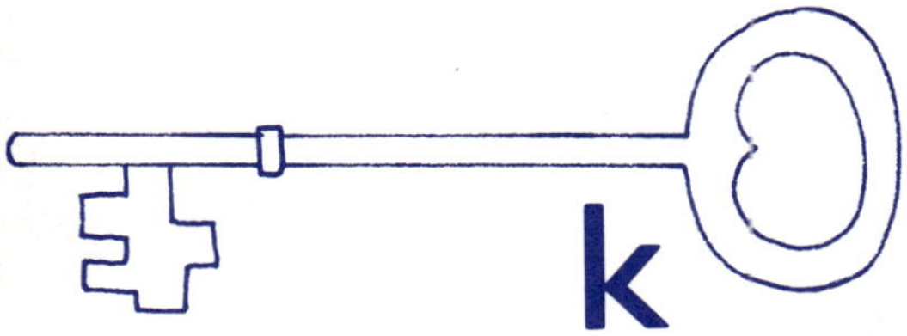

k ey

k ettle

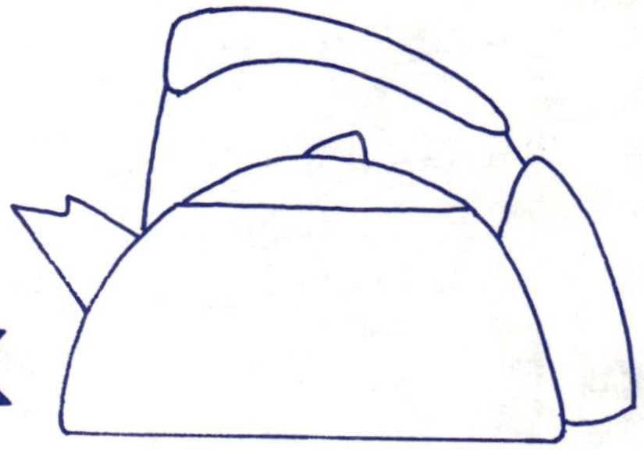

k ing

k ilt

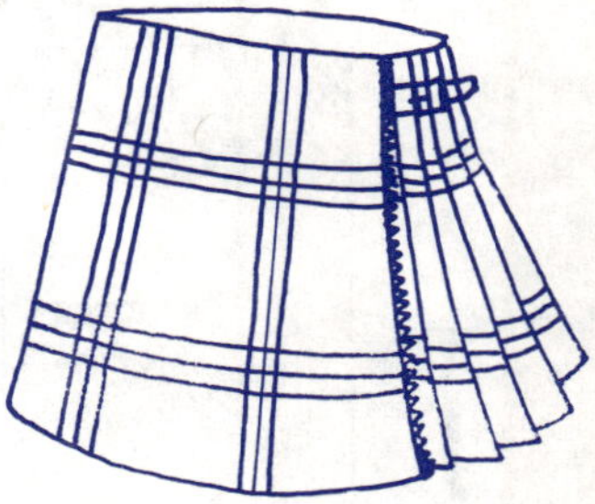

k

kicking kangaroo kissed the king

k ick

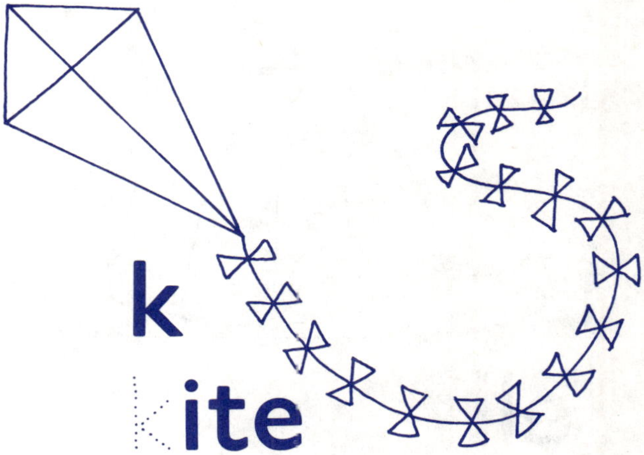

k ite

1 Talk about the pictures and repeat the words while listening for the **k** sound.
2 Trace the big **k** with a finger, then write **k** over the dotted letters. Read the word each time.
3 Read the phrase and learn it. Colour the pictures.
Further activities: 1 Make a **k** book. 2 Look for more **k** words, e.g. kingfisher, koala, kipper, kerb.

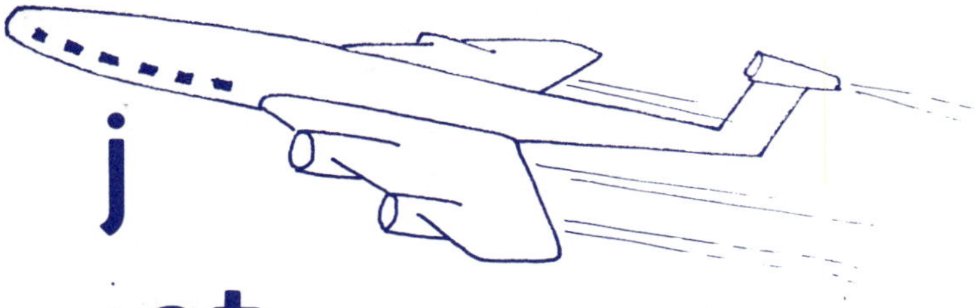

j et

j igsaw

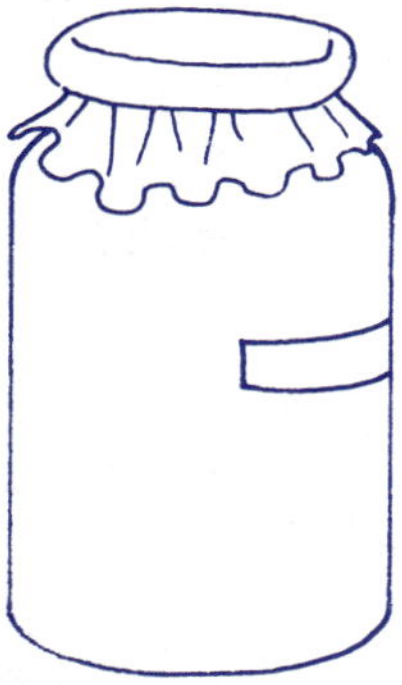

j am

j

j ug

jumping jackdaw judges jellies

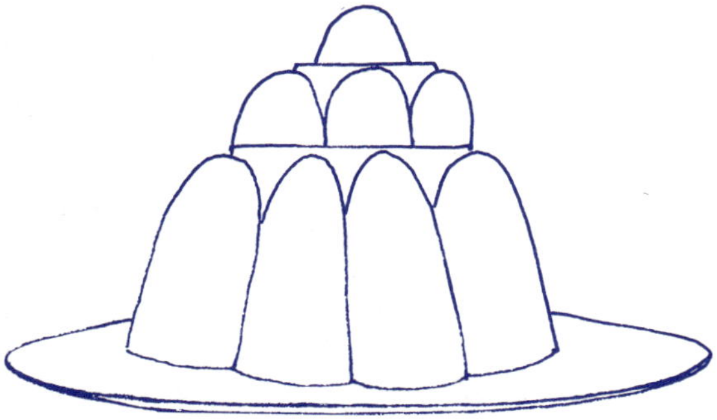

j elly

j acket

1 Talk about the pictures and repeat the words while listening for the **j** sound.
2 Trace the big **j** with a finger, then write **j** over the dotted letters. Read the word each time.
3 Read the phrase and learn it. Colour the pictures.

Further activities: 1 Make your own jigsaw by cutting up an old birthday card. 2 Make four labels – **j**, **r**, **k** and **s**. Hold them up one at a time, asking your child to do appropriate actions for each card, e.g. jump for **j**, run for **r**, kick for **k**, sit for **s**.

1 Talk about the pictures and repeat the words while listening for the **w** sound.
2 Trace the big **w** with a finger, then write **w** over the dotted letters. Read the word each time.
3 Read the phrase and learn it. Colour the pictures.

Further activities: 1 Make some cardboard worms and stick **w** pictures on them. Hang them from the ceiling. 2 Look out for **w** words, e.g. wafer, wellingtons, wizard, well, wish, week (no **wh** words).

Rhyming words

23

1 Look at the pictures on the first line and talk about them.

2 Say the words, asking your child to listen carefully. Say 'cat' again and find two words to rhyme with it along the line.

3 Do the same with each line, and colour the rhyming objects red.

Further activities: Make a large cat from two circles of card, and stick pictures of things rhyming with 'cat' onto it. Do the same for pan, fin, bun and jug.

Sounds at the beginning 24

1 Say the sound in the first line and name the object illustrated on the left.

2 Look for two objects beginning with that sound in the first line, and colour them blue. Write over the dotted letter.

3 Repeat this with each line.

Further activities: Make some letter snap cards by writing **h, j, k, w, b**, on card, 3 times each, making a total of 15 cards.

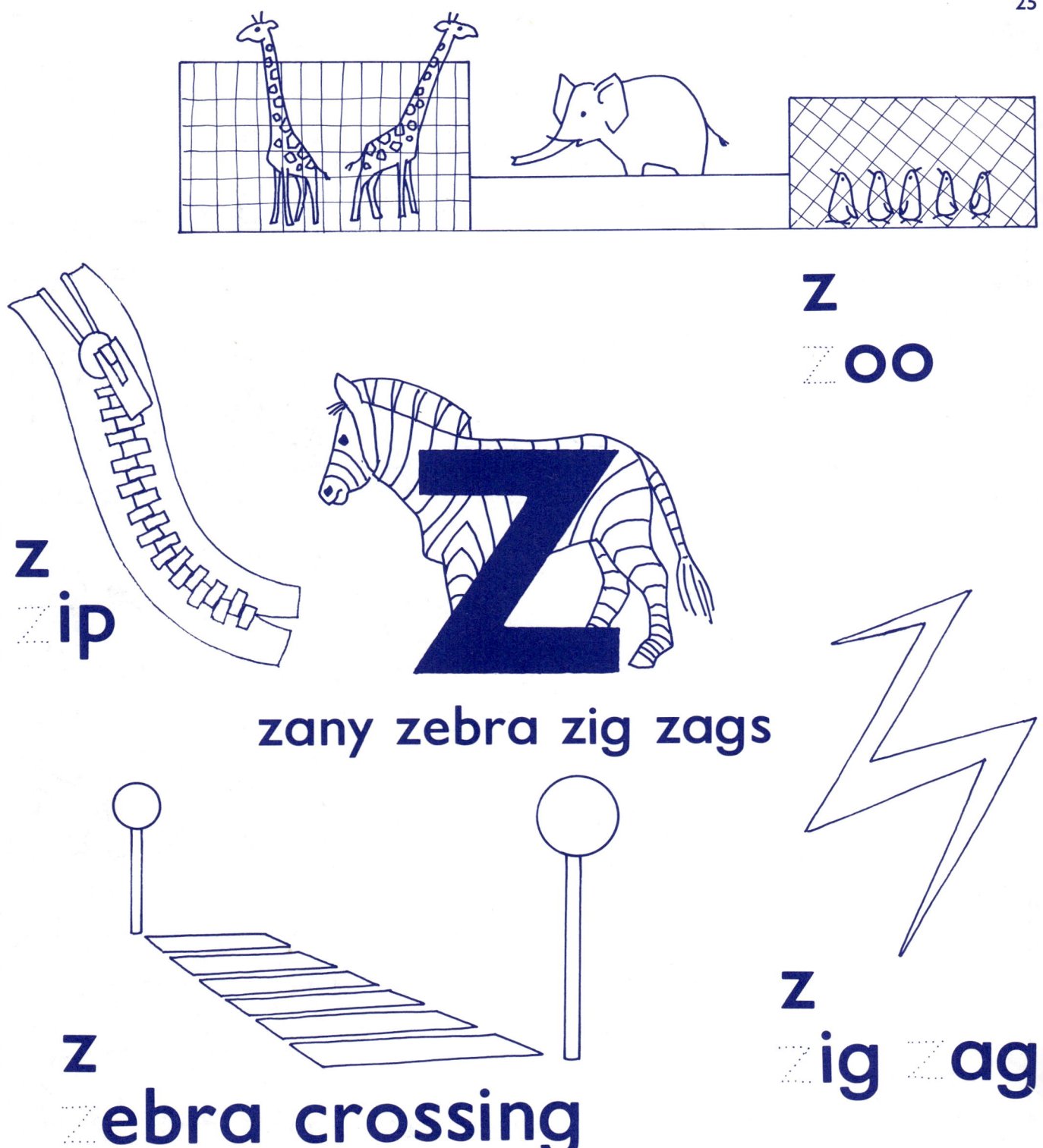

z
zoo

z
zip

zany zebra zig zags

z
zebra crossing

z
zig zag

1 Talk about the pictures and repeat the words while listening for the **z** sound.
2 Trace the big **z** with a finger, then write **z** over the dotted letters. Read the word each time.
3 Read the phrase and learn it. Colour the pictures.

Further activities: 1 Make some zig zags from newspaper and colour patterns on them. 2 Ask your child to walk, run, skip or jump in a zig zag saying 'zzzzz'.

vegetables

vase

violet

vile vulture visits villages

violin

van

vest

1 Talk about the pictures and repeat the words while listening for the **v** sound.
2 Trace the big **v** with a finger, then write **v** over the dotted letters. Read the word each time.
3 Read the phrase and learn it. Colour the pictures.
Further activities: 1 Make a **v** book.   2 Look for more **v** words, e.g. vet, volcano, visitor, vinegar, village.

27

yacht
yolk
yoghurt
yo-yo

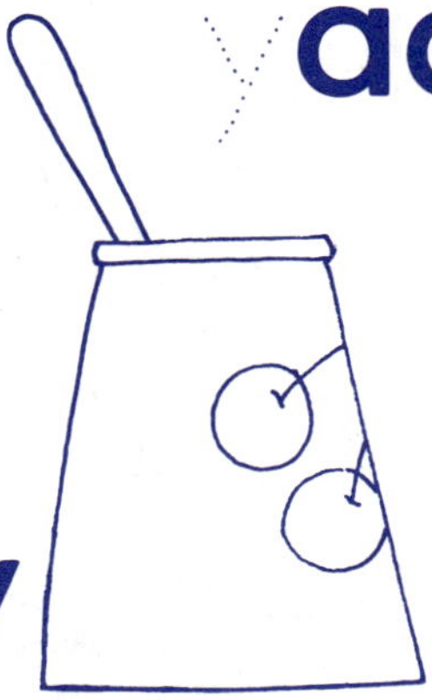

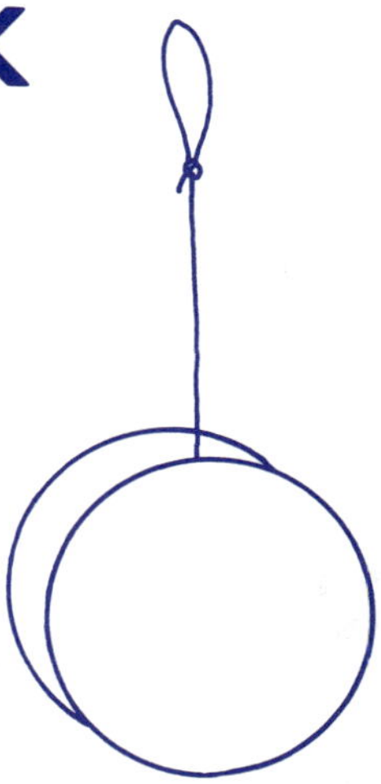

yellow yak yawned yesterday

yawn
yard

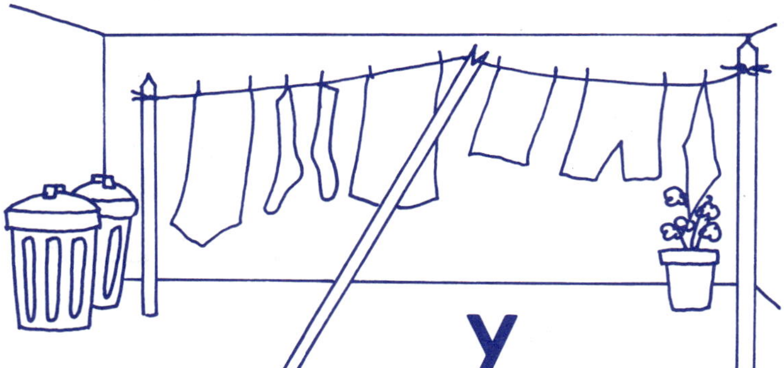

1 Talk about the pictures and repeat the words while listening for the y sound.
2 Trace the big **y** with a finger, then write **y** over the dotted letters. Read the word each time.
3 Read the phrase and learn it. Colour the pictures.

Further activities: **1** Make a yellow yak out of card. Write **y** on it and hang it from the ceiling. **2** Make a pattern of big **y**'s with paints or crayons. **3** Look for more **y** words, e.g. yes, yesterday, you, your, young, yap, year.

Beginning sounds

1 Talk about the picture and the objects illustrated. Ask questions, e.g. What is happening?
2 Find the beginning sounds for each of the objects – say the word and point to the sound. Then draw a line from each object to its sound.
3 Colour the picture.

In the supermarket

1 Talk about the picture and ask questions, e.g. Have you ever been in a supermarket? Is our supermarket like this one? What is different about it?

2 Talk about the sounds you could hear if you were standing in the shop, e.g. What is the baby doing?

3 Colour the picture.

Further activities: Make a big picture of a supermarket by cutting out pictures from magazines and sticking them on a large sheet of paper.

Sounds and pictures

30

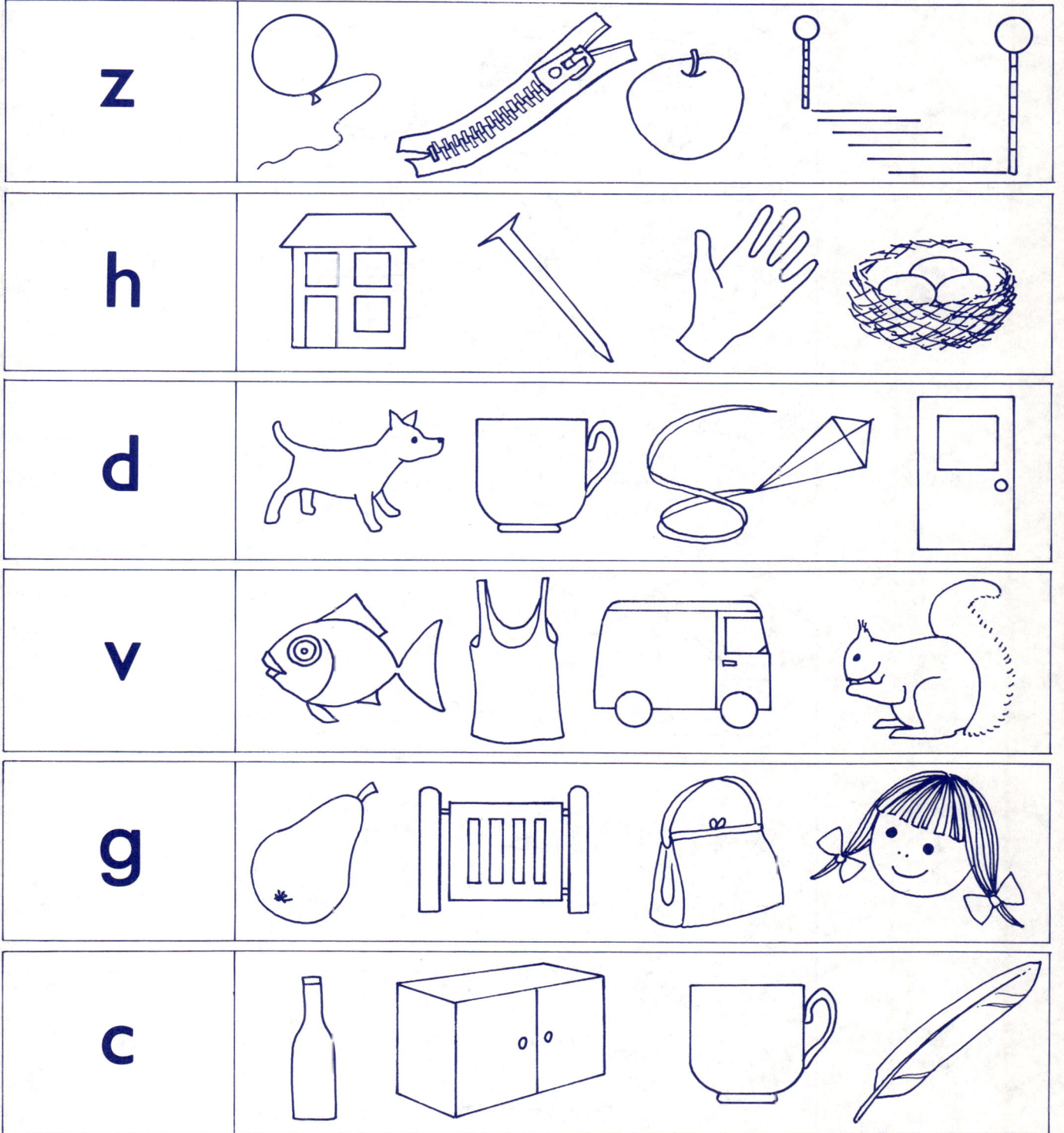

1 Say the sound in the first line. Repeat it.
2 Look for two objects beginning with that sound in the first line, and draw a ring round each one.
3 Repeat this with each line and colour the pictures.

Sounds and pictures

31

1 Say the sound in the first line. Repeat it.
2 Look for two objects beginning with that sound in the first line, and draw a ring round each one.
3 Repeat this with each line and colour the pictures.